"You start by practicing. And at first, you d just think 'how hard can it be?' Then you picl trim? It takes forever. Your hand's shaking, customer's sweating as much as you are. That ʒ ... hard it actually was until you tried."

I gestured at his fresh trim. "Then you do a few more. Each one teaches you something, how to hold the clippers at the right angle, where the natural hairline sits, how to blend without creating a line. You're still slow, still making mistakes, but now you *know* you're making mistakes.

That's the **Learning Stage**: You're aware of what you're getting wrong, and that awareness is progress. This is where most people give up"

"After maybe twenty, thirty cuts, something clicks. You start noticing what works. You try new tools, different guards, fading techniques. The cuts start taking shape. You're not fast yet, but you're not panicking either. You're thinking through each move deliberately.

That's the **Getting It Stage**: You can do it well, but you have to focus."

I paused. "Then one day, maybe after a hundred cuts, maybe two hundred, you stop thinking. Your hand just moves. The fade flows. You're chatting with the customer, making jokes, and your hands are doing their job without you having to tell them every step.

That's the **Mastery Stage**: The art of cutting hair becomes second nature."

"But here's the thing, you don't get to Mastery Stage by quitting at the Clueless or Learning Stages. If you'd given up on your first dodgy attempt because it wasn't perfect, you'd never have learned. Every bad fade I did, and trust me, I did a *few* bad fades, that was just training.

It took me at least six months of doing bad fades before I got decent. But I was determined to master the art. And eventually, I did."

He nodded slowly, and I could see the realization settling in.

"Job applications are the same. Your first CV? Clunky. Your first interview? Awkward. But every attempt moves you up those stages. Don't give up at the first Stage. Get to the Mastery Stage. That's where the 'yes' is waiting."

He laughed, but I could see something clicking.

"So why," I continued, "are you treating job applications like they're supposed to be perfect on the first try? You're not training. You're just hoping to get lucky."

Over the next few weeks, I couldn't stop thinking about that conversation. I started asking every young person who came through my door about their job search. The pattern was unmistakable:

The ones who were stuck had sent one, maybe two applications. They'd spent weeks crafting them, agonizing over every word, waiting for the "right" opportunity. And they were miserable.

The ones who were thriving? They were sending applications everywhere. Ten, fifteen, twenty a week. They weren't precious about it. They were treating it like practice. And you know what? They had options. Multiple interviews. Multiple offers. They got to *choose* what worked for them, location, pay, culture, growth potential. They weren't just grateful for any job; they were making strategic decisions about their lives.

That's when I realized:

Volume creates options, and options develop decision-making skills.

This isn't just barber shop philosophy. Turns out, there's a psychologist named Albert Bandura who spent his entire career studying how people build confidence. His research shows that confidence doesn't come from thinking positive thoughts or waiting until you feel ready. It comes from *mastery experiences*, doing the thing, getting feedback, adjusting, and doing it again. Over and over.

Every "no" you get isn't rejection. It's data. It's training. It's one rep closer to your eventual "yes."

But here's the thing nobody tells you: You need a lot of reps. Not two. Not five. A *lot*. Because volume doesn't just get you a job faster, it teaches you how to make better decisions. When you've only got one offer, you take it, even if it's rubbish. When you've got five offers, you get to ask yourself: What actually matters to me? Do I care more about money or a short commute? Do I want a big corporate environment or a small team where I'll learn faster? Do I prioritize stability or growth?

That's the skill nobody's teaching. We're so obsessed with getting young people *a* job that we forget to teach them how to choose a *good* job. And that skill, evaluating options, understanding your priorities, making strategic decisions, that's what sets you up for a satisfying life, not just a paycheck.

The Volume Experience Method

Every No Is Training For Your Yes

Errol Lloyd Jones

Contents

INTRODUCTION: THE BARBER'S DISCOVERY   IV

1. THE PASSENGER PROBLEM   1

2. THE "YET" REVOLUTION   7

3. WHY CAREER ADVICE FAILS   12

4. VOLUME CREATES MASTERY   18

5. THE POWER OF OPTIONS   24

6. PRACTICING DECISIONS   32

7. PARENT PARTNERSHIP   39

8. FROM NO TO KNOW   46

9. THE CONFIDENCE CURVE   52

10. FROM THEORY TO ACTION   60

ABOUT THE AUTHOR   70

RESOURCES   71

INTRODUCTION: THE BARBER'S DISCOVERY

Look, I've been cutting hair for 34 years, and I've heard every career sob story you can imagine. Kids come in here feeling defeated before they've even started, convinced they're not good enough, smart enough, or connected enough to get anywhere in life.

But here's what I figured out after thousands of these conversations: The advice we're giving young people about careers is not just wrong, it's the wrong way around. We tell them to craft the perfect CV, wait for the perfect opportunity, and apply only when they're 100% qualified. Meanwhile, they're sitting in my chair, three months after graduation, wondering why nothing's working.

That's when I discovered something that changed everything.

It was a Wednesday afternoon, this lad came in for a trim. Year 11, just finished his GCSEs, looking absolutely gutted. I asked him how the job search was going, and he said, "I applied for this apprenticeship at a garage. I really wanted it. They said no."

"How many other places have you applied?" I asked.

He looked at me like I'd asked him to solve quantum physics. "Just that one. I spent two weeks on the application. Made it perfect."

Two weeks. One application. And now he was done trying.

That's when it hit me. We've taught an entire generation to treat job applications like marriage proposals,something you only do when you're absolutely certain, when everything's perfect, when you've rehearsed every word. No wonder they're terrified. No wonder they're stuck.

I put down my clippers and said, "Mate, do you know how you learn to fade hair?"

He shrugged.

School gets you Exam-Ready at 16, and the Job Centre steps in at 18. That gives you two years to build experience in the single skill you'll need for the next decade and beyond—job seeking. And here's the secret: it's free. Job applications and interviews cost you nothing but time, so why not get as much practice as possible? Start applying.

So I built a platform. JumpstartCareers.co.uk. A place where young people could practice the Volume Experience Method, what I now call V.E.M. Ten applications a week. Track your pipeline. Build your CV. Practice interviews. Get feedback. Adjust. Repeat. And it works.

I've watched kids go from zero confidence to multiple offers in eight weeks. I've seen them learn to articulate what they want, negotiate better terms, and walk into jobs they actually chose rather than just accepted. I've seen parents stop nagging and start supporting. I've seen teachers use the data to prove their careers programs actually work.

But here's what I need you to understand: This book isn't about me. It's about a method that challenges everything you think you know about career preparation.

If you're a young person, this book will teach you that you're not broken, you're just undertrained. You'll learn how to generate options, figure out what matters to you, and make decisions that actually fit your life.

If you're a parent, this book will show you how to support your teen without taking over, how to ask the right questions instead of giving the wrong answers, and how to help them build decision-making skills that'll serve them for decades.

If you're an educator, this book will give you an evidence-based, measurable system that reduces your workload while improving outcomes. You'll see how VEM aligns with Gatsby Benchmarks, supports PSHE objectives, and gives you the data you need to prove your careers program works.

Here's my promise to you: By the end of this book, you'll never look at career preparation the same way again. You'll understand why "every 'no' is training for your eventual 'yes.'" You'll know how to turn frustration into fuel. You'll see why the word "yet" is the most powerful tool in your vocabulary. And you'll have a system, not just inspiration, but a genuine, replicable system, for building confidence, creating options, and making better decisions.

This isn't a theory. This is 34 years of conversations, thousands of success stories, and a method that's already changing lives across the UK. Let's get started.

Chapter One

THE PASSENGER PROBLEM

His name was Jayden. Sixteen years old, a bright kid, came in every six weeks for a trim. Always polite, always on his phone, always seemed a bit... elsewhere.

One day I asked him what he was up to after school. He shrugged. "Dunno. Probably college, I guess. Everyone else is going."

"What do you want to study?"

Another shrug. "Whatever. Doesn't really matter, does it? I'll just end up in some boring job anyway."

I stopped mid-fade. "You really believe that?"

He looked up from his phone for the first time. "I mean, yeah? That's just how it is. You go to school, you go to college, you get a job, you pay bills until you die. It's not like I get to choose."

There it was. The Passenger Problem.

Jayden wasn't depressed. He wasn't lazy. He wasn't even particularly pessimistic. He'd just accepted that life was something that happened *to* him, not something he had any control over. He was sitting in the back seat, watching the world go by, waiting for someone else to drive him somewhere.

And he wasn't alone.

I started paying attention, and I realized that most of the young people coming through my door had the same energy. Passive. Resigned. Going through the motions because that's what you're supposed to do, not because they'd chosen it.

They'd talk about their future the way you talk about the weather, something external, unpredictable, mostly out of your hands. "If I get into uni..." "If someone hires me..." "If I'm lucky..."

No agency. No ownership. Just... waiting.

And here's the thing that really got me: They weren't wrong to feel that way. The system had trained them to be passengers.

Think about it. From the time they're five years old, we tell kids where to sit, what to learn, when to eat, when to speak, when to be quiet. We test them on things they didn't choose to study. We rank them against each other. We tell them their future depends on grades they earn in subjects they might not care about.

Then, at sixteen, we suddenly expect them to become self-directed, motivated, strategic decision-makers. We hand them a careers questionnaire and say, "Right, what do you want to do with your life?"

Is it any wonder they shrug?

But here's what I've learned after 34 years of watching this pattern: People don't stay passengers forever. Eventually, something shifts. Something pisses them off enough that they decide to grab the wheel.

I call it the **P.O.P Algorithm**. And yeah, it stands for: **Pissed Off Passenger.**

Every driver was once a pissed off passenger.

You don't try anything new until you're really, truly fed up with your present state. Not mildly annoyed. Not vaguely dissatisfied. *Pissed off*.

That moment when you've had enough, when the frustration outweighs the fear, when staying where you are becomes more painful than the risk of trying something different.

That's the ignition point. That's when people take ***ACTION***.

Finding Your P.O.P Moment

Here's the thing about frustration: it's fuel. Pure, high-octane fuel that'll push you over any hill you've been staring at.

Take learning to drive. Not the fantasy version where you pass your test and cruise into the sunset. The real version.

You know what actually makes someone book driving lessons? It's not the appeal of freedom. It's standing at the bus stop in the pouring rain. Again. It's being the last one at the party waiting for your dad to pick you up. It's watching £15 disappear on a taxi for a journey that takes ten minutes. It's missing out on a job because the buses don't run early enough.

And suddenly you're thinking: lessons, car, insurance, MOT, repairs, fuel, parking, yeah, that's a massive hill to climb. But you know what's bigger? Another Saturday night stuck at home because you can't get anywhere.

When you're genuinely pissed off, when the discomfort of staying in your situtation exceeds the fear of moving forward, that mountain doesn't look so impossible anymore. You find the money for lessons. You save for a cheap motor. You stomach the insurance costs. You learn to budget for petrol.

The hill hasn't gotten smaller. You've just gotten fed up enough to climb it.

That's the secret: *anything* is conquerable if your "why" is strong enough. And your "why" is usually born from pure frustration.

Living at home and feeling suffocated? That's fuel. Stuck in a dead-end relationship? Fuel. Grinding away at a job you hate? Fuel. Relying on everyone else's schedule to get anywhere? Fuel.

The frustration isn't the problem. The frustration is the *solution*. It's what pushes you from passenger to driver.

You just have to get pissed off enough.

Jayden's P.O.P Moment

Let me tell you what happened with Jayden.

Three months after that first conversation, he came back in. Different energy entirely. He sat down, looked me straight in the eye, and said,

"I need to talk to you about getting a job."

"What changed?" I asked.

"My mum," he said. "She's been working at the same supermarket for fifteen years. I hate it. She comes home every day complaining. And last week she told me I should just apply there because 'at least it's stable.'

And I thought... I don't want that.

I don't want to spend my whole life doing something I hate just because it's stable."

There it was. The P.O.P moment.

Jayden wasn't pissed off at his mum, he was pissed off at the idea of *becoming* his mum. He'd seen his future as a passenger, and he didn't like the destination.

"So what do you want to do about it?" I asked.

"I don't know yet," he said. "But I want to figure it out. I want to actually choose."

That's the thing about P.O.P moments. They don't give you all the answers. They just give you the energy to start looking.

Over the next few weeks, Jayden and I worked through what I now call the VEM system. He started sending applications,not one perfect application, but ten a week. Retail, hospitality, admin, anything that sounded remotely interesting. He wasn't trying to find the perfect job; he was trying to create options.

And here's what happened: He got rejected. A lot. But he also got responses. Interview invitations. Offers.

By week six, he had three offers on the table. Three. And for the first time in his life, he got to ask himself: *What do I actually want?*

One job paid more but had a 90-minute commute. One was closer but felt a bit corporate and cold when he visited. One paid the least but had a small, friendly team and offered training he was actually interested in.

He picked the third one. Not because it was the "best" job objectively, but because it fit *his* priorities. He'd moved from passenger to driver.

Six months later, he came back in for a trim, and I asked how the job was going.

"I love it," he said. "And you know what's weird? Two of my friends took the supermarket job my mum suggested. They're already miserable. But they act like that's just how jobs are. And I'm like... no. You just didn't give yourself any options."

That's the Passenger Problem in a nutshell. When you don't create options, you don't get to choose. And when you don't get to choose, you end up wherever life drops you.

But here's the good news: You can get out of the passenger seat anytime you want. You don't need permission. You don't need perfect grades or a flawless CV or connections in high places.

You just need to get pissed off enough to try.

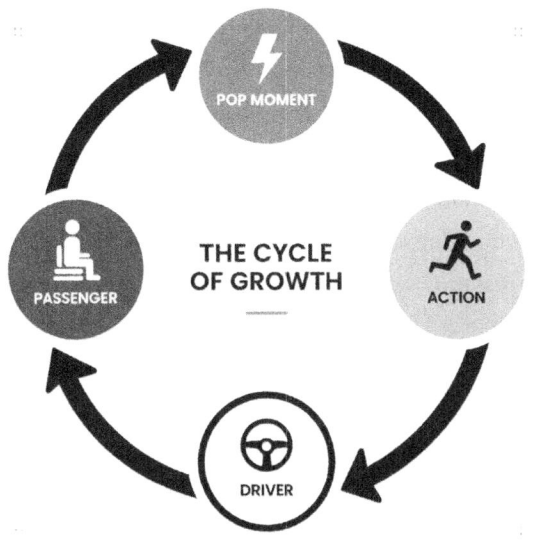

The P.O.P Cycle of Growth - Continuous transformation cycle

What This Means for You

If you're reading this and thinking, "Yeah, I'm definitely a passenger right now," that's okay. Most people are. The question is: Are you pissed off enough to do something about it?

Here's how you know you're ready for a P.O.P moment:

- You're tired of watching other people get opportunities while you wait for yours.

- You're frustrated that you're doing what you're "supposed" to do, but it's not working.

- You're scared of ending up in a life you didn't choose.

- You're starting to realize that nobody's coming to rescue you, you have to rescue yourself.

If any of that resonates, good. Use it. That frustration is fuel.

For parents: Your job isn't to create the P.O.P moment for your teen. You can't manufacture genuine frustration. But you can recognize it when it happens and help them channel it into action instead of despair. When your kid comes to you angry about their situation, don't try to fix it or calm them down. Ask: "What do you want to do about it?" That's the question that turns passengers into drivers.

For educators: The Passenger Problem is why so many of your students seem disengaged. They've been told what to do for so long that they've stopped believing they have any control. Your job is to create opportunities for them to make real choices, not fake choices like "pick a topic for your essay," but real ones like "here are five potential paths; which one do you want to explore?" When students experience genuine agency, even in small ways, they start to wake up.

The Passenger Problem isn't a character flaw. It's a learned behavior. And anything that's learned can be unlearned.

But first, you have to get pissed off enough to try.

Chapter Two

THE "YET" REVOLUTION

I didn't invent the word "yet." But I did figure out what it really means.

It started with a lad named Connor. Seventeen, just finished college, looking for work. He came in one day and said, "I can't do interviews."

Not "I'm not good at interviews." Not "I struggle with interviews." He said, "*I can't* do interviews."

I asked him how much he'd done.

"Two," he said. "Both disasters. I just froze up. I'm not an interview person."

Two. He'd done two interviews, decided he was fundamentally incapable, and was ready to write off his entire future based on that.

I put down my scissors and said, "You can't do interviews *yet*."

He looked at me like I'd just told him the earth was flat.

"What's the difference?" he asked.

"Massive difference," I said. "When you say 'I can't do interviews,' you're saying it's permanent. You're broken. There's no point trying. But when you say 'I can't do interviews *yet*,' you're saying it's temporary. You just haven't learned how. Yet."

He thought about that for a second. "Okay, but I still can't do them."

"Right. *Yet.* So what are you going to do about it?"

That question, *what are you going to do about it?*, is the whole point of "yet." It's not just a word you tack onto the end of a sentence to feel better. It's a commitment. It's a plan. It's the difference between giving up and getting started.

I told Connor, "You know what 'Y.E.T' stands for? **You'll Eventually Try.**"

He laughed. "That's cheesy."

"Yeah, it is. But it's also true. You can't do interviews yet, which means you'll eventually try again. And again. And again. Until you can."

Connor didn't look convinced, but he agreed to give it a shot. We set up mock interviews. I asked him the standard questions,tell me about yourself, what are your strengths, why do you want this job, and I recorded him on my phone so he could watch himself back.

The first one was rough. He mumbled. He said "um" about forty times. He forgot half of what he wanted to say.

But here's the thing: He didn't say "I can't do this." He said, "I can't do this *yet.*"

And that tiny word changed everything.

Because "yet" doesn't let you off the hook. It doesn't say, "Oh well, maybe someday." It says, "Not now, but soon. Keep going."

By the fifth mock interview, Connor was decent. By the tenth, he was good. By the fifteenth, he was confident. And when he went to his next real interview, he got the job.

A few weeks later, he came back in and said, "I can do interviews now."

"Yeah," I said. "You could always do them. You just couldn't do them *yet.*"

Why "Yet" Isn't Just Positive Thinking

Look, I'm not a fan of toxic positivity. You know the type, people who tell you to "just believe in yourself" and "manifest your dreams" and act like wanting something badly enough will make it happen.

That's nonsense. Believing you can do something doesn't make you able to do it. Wishing doesn't build skills.

But "yet" is different. "Yet" isn't about belief. It's about *action.*

When you say "I can't do something *yet,*" you're not lying to yourself. You're acknowledging reality: Right now, at this moment, you genuinely can't do it. But you're also acknowledging a second reality: Skills can be learned. You're not fixed. You're in progress.

And that second reality is what makes all the difference.

There's a researcher named Carol Dweck who spent decades studying what she calls "growth mindset" versus "fixed mindset." People with a fixed mindset believe their abilities are set in stone, you're either smart or you're not, talented or you're not, good at interviews or you're not. People with a growth mindset believe abilities can be developed through effort and practice.

Guess which group does better in life?

Dweck's research shows that people with a growth mindset take on harder challenges, persist longer when things get tough, and ultimately achieve more, not because they're more talented, but because they believe effort matters.

"Yet" is the language of growth mindset. It's the word that turns "I can't" into "I'm learning."

But here's where I think Dweck's research misses something important:

Growth mindset without action is just wishful thinking.

You can believe you'll eventually learn to do interviews, but if you never practice, you won't. You can believe you'll eventually get a job, but if you never apply, you won't.

That's why I say "yet" stands for **You'll Eventually Try.** It's not enough to believe you can grow. You have to actually do the work.

The "Yet" Transformation in Action

Once I figured out the power of "yet," I started using it with every young person who came through my door. And I started noticing patterns.

The kids who said "I can't" without "yet" stayed stuck. They'd come in month after month with the same problems, the same complaints, the same lack of progress. They'd blame the system, the economy, bad luck, other people. And yeah, sometimes those things were real factors. But mostly, they were stuck because they'd decided they couldn't move.

The kids who added "yet" to their vocabulary? They moved. Fast.

"I can't write a good CV *yet*" became "I wrote a decent CV and got three interview requests."

"I don't have any experience *yet*" became "I volunteered for two weeks and now I've got something to talk about."

"I don't know what I want to do *yet*" became "I tried three different things and figured out I actually like working with people."

It wasn't magic. It was just a shift in language that led to a shift in behavior.

Here's a real example. A boy named Aaron came in and said, "I can't get a job because I don't have experience, but I can't get experience because no one will hire me."

Classic catch-22. And he was right, it *is* harder to get your first job when you've got nothing on your CV.

But I asked him, "Can you get experience *yet*?"

He paused. "What do you mean?"

"I mean, right now, today, you don't have formal work experience. But could you get some? Could you volunteer somewhere? Could you help out at a local shop on weekends? Could you do a week's work experience through school?"

"I guess," he said. "But that's not a real job."

"No," I agreed. "But it's an experience. And experience is what you need to get a real job. So right now, you can't get hired *yet*. But you can get experience. And once you've got experience, you can get hired."

He thought about it. Then he said, "Okay. I'll try."

Two weeks later, he came back and told me he'd signed up to volunteer at a charity shop on Saturdays. A month after that, he'd updated his CV with his new "experience." Two months after that, he had a part-time job at a café.

"I can't believe that actually worked," he said.

"It worked because you added 'yet,'" I told him. "And then you did something about it."

What This Means for You

If you want to use "yet" effectively, here's how:

Step 1: Identify your "I can't" statements. What are you telling yourself you can't do? Write them down. Be honest.

Step 2: Add "yet" to every single one. Don't skip this step. Physically say the word out loud or write it down. "I can't do interviews *yet*." "I don't have experience *yet*." "I don't know what I want *yet*."

Step 3: Ask yourself: What's one small thing I could try this week? Not a massive life-changing action. Just one small thing. One application. One conversation. One Google search. One volunteer shift.

Step 4: Do it. This is the part where most people get stuck. They add "yet," they feel a bit better, and then they don't actually do anything. Don't be that person. "Yet" without action is just procrastination with better grammar.

For parents: When your teen says "I can't," resist the urge to immediately reassure them or solve the problem. Instead, ask: "Can you do it *yet*?" And then: "What's one small thing you could try?" Your job is to help them see the gap between "not now" and "eventually" as a space they can fill with effort, not a permanent wall.

For educators: "Yet" is one of the most powerful words you can teach. But don't just tell students to say it, build it into your feedback. Instead of "This essay isn't good enough," try "This essay isn't good enough *yet*, here's what to work on." Instead of "You're not ready for that," try "You're not ready *yet*, here's how to get ready." Language shapes belief, and belief shapes behavior.

"Yet" isn't a magic word. But it is a powerful one. Because it takes the fixed, permanent, hopeless feeling of "I can't" and turns it into the temporary, solvable, actionable reality of "I'm learning."

And learning is something anyone can do.

You just have to try.

Chapter Three

WHY CAREER ADVICE FAILS

L et me tell you about the worst piece of career advice I ever heard.

A lad came into the shop, maybe eighteen, looking stressed. I asked him what was up, and he said, "I've been working on my CV for three weeks, and it's still not good enough."

Three weeks. On a CV. For someone with no work experience.

"Who told you it needs to be perfect?" I asked.

"Everyone," he said. "My careers advisor said I only get one shot at a first impression, so I need to make sure it's flawless. My mum said employers get hundreds of applications, so mine has to stand out. My mate said if there's even one typo, they'll bin it immediately."

So this kid had spent three weeks agonizing over a single piece of paper, terrified to send it anywhere because it might not be perfect. And in those three weeks, he'd applied to exactly zero jobs.

That's when I realized: **Traditional career advice is designed to make you fail.**

Not intentionally, obviously. The people giving this advice mean well. They genuinely believe they're helping. But the advice itself, "perfect your CV," "only apply to jobs you're 100% qualified for," "wait for the right opportunity", is fundamentally broken.

Here's why.

The "Quality Over Quantity" Myth

We've all heard it: "It's better to send one great application than ten mediocre ones."

Sounds reasonable, right? Focus your energy. Make every application count. Show employers you really care.

Except it's completely wrong.

Here's what actually happens when you follow that advice:

You spend days crafting the perfect CV. You research the company extensively. You write a tailored cover letter that references specific details from their website. You proofread seventeen times. You ask three people to review it. You finally send it off, feeling proud of the work you've done.

And then... nothing.

Maybe they don't respond at all. Maybe you get a generic rejection email two weeks later. Either way, you've just spent days on something that went nowhere.

Now you're demoralized. You're questioning whether you're good enough. You're wondering if you should spend another week perfecting your CV before trying again.

Meanwhile, the kid who sent ten "mediocre" applications? They've got three interview requests.

Because here's the truth nobody tells you: **Employers don't reject you because your application isn't perfect. They reject you because they've got fifty other applicants and they can only interview five.**

Your application could be flawless, and you'd still get rejected. Not because you're not good enough, but because the numbers don't work in your favor.

So what's the solution? **Change the numbers.**

If you send one perfect application and you've got a 10% chance of getting an interview, you'll probably get nothing. If you send ten decent applications and you've got a 10% chance on each one, you'll probably get one interview. If you send twenty, you'll get two.

This isn't about being sloppy. It's about understanding that job searching is a numbers game, and the only way to win a numbers game is to play it.

But traditional career advice tells you the opposite. It tells you to spend all your time perfecting one application instead of sending many. It prioritizes the *process* over the *outcome*. And it leaves young people stuck, polishing a CV that's never quite good enough to send.

The Paralysis of Perfection

There's a term in psychology called "analysis paralysis." It's when you overthink something so much that you can't make a decision.

Traditional career advice creates analysis paralysis on an industrial scale.

"Make sure your CV is perfect." Okay, but what does perfect mean? Should I use bullet points or paragraphs? One page or two? Should I include my GCSEs if I've got A-levels? Should I mention hobbies? What if my hobbies sound boring? What if they sound too interesting and the employer thinks I'll be distracted?

"Only apply to jobs you're qualified for." Okay, but the job description says they want two years of experience and I've got none. Does my volunteer work count? What about the time I helped my uncle with his shop? Should I apply anyway, or will that make me look desperate?

"Wait for the right opportunity." Okay, but how do I know if it's the right opportunity? What if I take this job and then a better one comes along next week? What if I turn this one down and nothing else comes up?

These questions are endless. And the more you think about them, the more paralyzed you become.

I see this all the time. Young people who are smart, capable, and hardworking, but they're stuck because they're trying to make the "right" decision. They're waiting for clarity that never comes.

Here's what I tell them: **You don't need the right decision. You need a decision.**

Because here's the thing about decisions: You learn more from making them than from avoiding them. Even if you make the "wrong" choice, you'll learn something. You'll learn what you don't like. You'll learn what matters to you. You'll learn how to evaluate your next choice better.

But if you never make a choice because you're waiting for perfect information, you learn nothing. You just stay stuck.

Traditional career advice tells you to wait until you're ready. But you'll never feel ready. Ready is a feeling you get *after* you've done the thing, not before.

The Academic vs Real-World Gap

Here's another problem with traditional career advice: It's written by people who haven't applied for an entry-level job in twenty years.

I'm not saying careers advisors and teachers don't care. They absolutely do. But most of them got their jobs in a completely different economy, with completely different expectations, and they're giving advice based on what worked for them.

And what worked for them doesn't work anymore.

Twenty years ago, you could walk into a shop, ask if they were hiring, and hand them a CV. Now, everything's online. You're not talking to a person; you're filling out a form that gets filtered by software before a human ever sees it.

Twenty years ago, staying in one job for your entire career was normal. Now, young people are expected to be "flexible" and "adaptable," which is code for "you'll probably have five different jobs in your twenties and that's fine."

Twenty years ago, a degree was a golden ticket. Now, half of graduates are in jobs that don't require a degree, and they're competing with people who've got three years of work experience instead of three years of student debt.

The world has changed. But the advice hasn't.

I see this gap every day. A careers advisor tells a kid, "Just show up in person and introduce yourself, it shows initiative!" The kid does that, and the manager says, "We don't accept walk-ins. Apply online."

A teacher tells a kid, "Get a degree and you'll be fine." The kid gets a degree, graduates with £40,000 in debt, and can't find a job because every entry-level position wants two years of experience.

A parent tells a kid, "Just work hard and you'll get ahead." The kid works hard, gets good grades, does everything right, and still ends up competing with a hundred other people for the same job.

It's not that the advice is malicious. It's just outdated. And outdated advice is worse than no advice, because it makes you feel like you're doing the right thing when you're actually wasting your time.

What the Statistics Actually Tell Us

Let's talk numbers for a second, because this is where traditional career advice really falls apart.

In the UK, youth unemployment sits at around 14.2%. That's nearly one in seven young people who want to work but can't find a job. And that's just the official number, it doesn't include people who've given up looking, or people who are underemployed, working part-time when they want full-time.

Surveys show that 62% of young people find job hunting difficult. Not just annoying or time-consuming, *difficult*. As in, they don't know how to do it effectively.

And here's the kicker: The average job posting gets 118 applications. One hundred and eighteen. For every single job.

So when traditional career advice tells you to "make your application stand out," what they're really saying is: "Be better than 117 other people."

How are you supposed to do that when you're sixteen with no experience?

You can't. Not with one perfect application.

But you know what you *can* do? You can apply to ten jobs. Twenty jobs. Fifty jobs. You can play the numbers game. You can get good at applications by doing a lot of them. You can learn what works and what doesn't through trial and error.

And here's the thing: The kids who do that? They're the ones who get jobs.

I've got data from my platform, JumpstartCareers.co.uk, that proves it. Students who send fewer than five applications a month have about a 12% chance of getting an interview. Students who send ten or more applications a week? Their interview rate jumps to over 40%.

It's not because they're better candidates. It's because they're giving themselves more chances.

Traditional career advice ignores this reality. It tells you to focus on quality, to wait for the right opportunity, and to be patient. And while you're being patient, someone else is sending twenty applications and getting three interviews.

What This Means for You

If you've been following traditional career advice and it's not working, it's not because you're doing it wrong. It's because the advice is wrong.

Here's what you should do instead:

Stop trying to perfect your CV. Get it to "good enough" and start sending it. You'll learn more from ten responses (or ten rejections) than you will from ten more hours of editing.

Stop waiting for the right opportunity. There's no such thing. Every job teaches you something, even if it's just "I don't want to do this long-term." Apply widely. Create options. Figure out what you want by trying things, not by thinking about them.

Stop listening to people who haven't job-searched recently. I don't care if they're well-meaning. If they haven't applied for a job in the last five years, their advice is probably outdated. Find people who've recently been through the process and ask them what actually worked.

For parents: I know you want to protect your kids from rejection and failure. But when you tell them to "wait for the right job" or "make sure everything's perfect first," you're accidentally teaching them to be afraid. The best thing you can do is encourage them to try, fail, learn, and try again. That's how resilience is built.

For educators: Please, *please* stop teaching students that there's one right way to do a CV or one right answer to "where do you see yourself in five years?" The real world is messy and unpredictable, and the students who succeed are the ones who can adapt, not the ones who follow a script. Teach them to experiment. Teach them that rejection is data, not failure. Teach them that volume creates options.

Traditional career advice fails because it's built on outdated assumptions about how the world works. It assumes there's a clear path, a right way, a perfect strategy.

There isn't.

But there is a better way. And it starts with letting go of perfection and embracing volume.

Chapter Four

VOLUME CREATES MASTERY

A lright, let's talk about the thing that changes everything: **volume.**

Not quality. Not perfection. Not waiting for the right moment.

Volume.

I know that sounds counterintuitive. We've been taught our whole lives that quality matters more than quantity, that you should focus your energy, that trying too many things means you're not committed.

But when it comes to building confidence and creating opportunities, volume is the secret.

Let me show you why.

The 10-Per-Week Rule

A few years ago, I started tracking the young people I was working with. I wanted to know: What actually predicts success? Is it grades? Is it confidence? Is it having a great CV?

Turns out, none of those things mattered as much as one simple metric: **How many applications are you sending per week?**

Kids who sent fewer than five applications a month? Most of them were still looking for work three months later.

Kids who sent five to ten applications a month? About half of them found something within two months.

Kids who sent ten or more applications *per week*? Nearly all of them had multiple offers within six to eight weeks.

Ten per week. That's the magic number.

Not because ten is some mystical threshold, but because ten is enough to create momentum. It's enough that you stop treating each application like a life-or-death decision. It's enough that you start to see patterns,what works, what doesn't, what gets responses, what gets ignored.

And most importantly, it's enough to create *options*.

Because here's the thing: When you've only got one offer, you take it. You don't ask questions. You don't negotiate. You don't evaluate whether it's actually a good fit. You just say yes, because what choice do you have?

But when you've got three offers? Five offers? Suddenly, you're in control. You get to ask yourself: Which one pays better? Which one has a shorter commute? Which one has a team I actually like? Which one offers training I'm interested in?

You get to *choose*. And that ability to choose,that's what builds confidence. That's what teaches you decision-making skills. That's what sets you up for long-term success.

How Volume Builds Confidence

There's a psychologist named Albert Bandura who spent his career studying something called *self-efficacy*,basically, your belief in your ability to succeed at something.

Bandura found that self-efficacy comes from four sources:

1. **Mastery experiences** – Actually doing the thing and succeeding.

2. **Vicarious experiences** – Watching someone else do it and thinking, "If they can, I can."

3. **Verbal persuasion** – Someone you trust telling you that you can do it.

4. **Managing your emotional state** – Learning to calm your nerves and stay focused.

Of those four, mastery experiences are by far the most powerful. Nothing builds confidence like actually doing the thing.

But here's the catch: You can't have a mastery experience if you never try. And you can't build real confidence from one success, because one success could be luck.

You need *repeated* success. You need to do the thing over and over, see that it works, and internalize the belief that you're capable.

That's what volume does.

When you send one application and get rejected, it feels personal. You think, "I'm not good enough."

When you send ten applications and get rejected from nine, it feels like math. You think, "Okay, my hit rate is about 10%. I need to send more."

When you send fifty applications and get five interviews, you start to see the pattern. You realize that rejection isn't about you,it's about fit, timing, and numbers. And you start to feel confident because you know that if you keep going, you'll get results.

That's mastery. Not from being perfect, but from doing the reps.

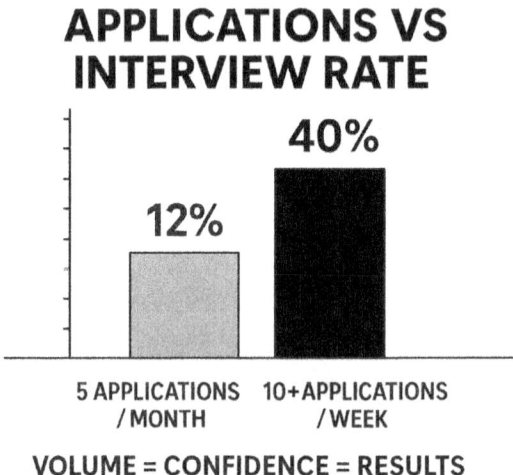

Volume Creates Results - Traditional vs VEM application rates

The Decision-Making Development Strategy

But volume isn't just about getting *a* job. It's about learning to choose a *good* job.

This is the part that most career advice completely misses.

Everyone's so focused on helping young people get hired that they forget to teach them how to evaluate opportunities. And that's a massive problem, because the ability to make good decisions,about jobs, about education, about life,is one of the most important skills you can have.

Here's how volume teaches decision-making:

Stage 1: Volume creates options. You send ten applications a week. You get responses. You get interviews. You get offers. Suddenly, you're not desperate,you're evaluating.

Stage 2: Options force you to clarify your priorities. When you've only got one offer, you don't have to think about what matters to you. But when you've got three offers, you have to ask: Do I care more about money or location? Do I want a big company or a small team? Do I prioritize learning opportunities or work-life balance?

Stage 3: Priorities guide your choices. Once you know what matters to you, you can evaluate your options strategically. You're not just taking whatever comes first,you're choosing the best fit.

Stage 4: Choices create ownership. When you make a decision based on your priorities, you own it. It's not something that happened to you; it's something you chose. And that sense of ownership builds confidence and resilience.

Stage 5: Ownership leads to satisfaction. When you're in a job you chose because it aligns with your priorities, you're more likely to stick with it, work hard, and feel good about it. Even if it's not perfect, it's *yours*.

This is the strategy that nobody teaches. We tell young people to "find their passion" or "follow their dreams," but we don't teach them how to actually evaluate options and make strategic decisions.

Volume does that. Because you can't learn to choose if you don't have choices.

Real Success Stories

Let me tell you about a lad named Marcus.

Marcus came to me halfway through Year 11, stressed out of his mind. He wanted to be a mechanic, but every apprenticeship he looked at wanted experience. And he couldn't get experience because no one would hire him without experience.

Classic catch-22.

I told him, "Stop looking for the perfect apprenticeship. Start applying everywhere. Garages, dealerships, tire shops, MOT centers. Anywhere that touches cars. Ten applications a week."

He looked at me like I was mad. "But most of those aren't apprenticeships."

"Doesn't matter," I said. "You need to get your foot in the door. You need to show someone you're willing to work. Once you're in, you can figure out the next step."

He didn't love the idea, but he tried it. And within three weeks, he had a Saturday job at a tire shop. Not an apprenticeship. Not glamorous. But it was *something*.

Two months later, the shop owner mentioned that a local garage was looking for an apprentice. Marcus applied, mentioned his tire shop experience, and got the apprenticeship.

Would that have happened if he'd kept waiting for the perfect opportunity? No. He'd still be sitting at home, polishing his CV, hoping someone would take a chance on him.

But because he created volume,because he applied widely and took what was available,he created options. And those options led to the outcome he actually wanted.

Here's another one. A boy named Preston.

Preston had no idea what he wanted to do. He liked people, he liked organizing things, but he didn't have a specific career in mind. So I told him, "Apply to ten different types of jobs. Retail, hospitality, admin, customer service, events. Just try things."

He thought I was joking. "You want me to apply for jobs I don't even want?"

"I want you to apply for jobs you *might* want," I said. "You don't know what you like until you try it."

So he did. And over the next two months, he got interviews in five different sectors. He tried a weekend shift in retail,and hated it. He tried a week of work experience in an office,which was boring. He tried a shift at a café,loved it.

He ended up taking a job in hospitality, and six months later, he told me, "I never would have guessed I'd like this. But I actually love it. I love the pace, I love the people, I love that every day is different."

He only figured that out because he tried multiple things. If he'd waited to "find his passion" before applying anywhere, he'd still be waiting.

That's what volume does. It turns uncertainty into clarity. It turns "I don't know" into "I tried five things and now I know."

What This Means for You

If you take one thing from this chapter, let it be this: **Volume is not about being desperate. It's about being strategic.**

You're not applying everywhere because you'll take anything. You're applying everywhere because you're creating options, building skills, and learning what you actually want.

Here's how to put this into practice:

Set a weekly target. Ten applications per week. It sounds like a lot, but it's less than two per day. You can do that.

Track your numbers. How many applications did you send? How many responses did you get? How many interviews? This isn't about judging yourself, it's about seeing the pattern. If you send ten and get one interview, great. Now you know your hit rate. Send twenty next week and you'll get two.

Celebrate the reps, not just the results. Every application you send is a win, even if you get rejected. You're training. You're building the habit. You're creating opportunities.

Use rejection as data. If you're getting lots of rejections, look for patterns. Are you applying to jobs that are too senior? Is your CV missing key information? Are you not following up? Adjust and try again.

For parents: Stop asking your teen, "Have you heard back yet?" and start asking, "How many applications did you send this week?" Shift the focus from outcomes (which they can't control) to effort (which they can). And when they get rejected, don't try to make them feel better. Just say, "Okay, what's next?"

For educators: Build volume into your careers program. Don't just teach students how to write a CV, give them a target. Ten applications by the end of the term. Track it. Celebrate it. Make it normal to apply widely, get rejected often, and keep going.

Volume creates mastery. Mastery creates confidence. Confidence creates options. Options create good decisions. Good decisions create satisfying lives.

It all starts with doing the reps.

So stop waiting. Stop perfecting. Stop hoping for the right opportunity to appear.

Start sending. Start trying. Start building.

Because every "no" is training for your eventual "yes."

And the more reps you do, the sooner that "yes" comes.

Chapter Five

THE POWER OF OPTIONS

Why More Applications Unlock Better Futures

There's a moment I'll never forget. A lad named Tyler, nineteen years old, sitting in my chair with the biggest grin I'd ever seen on him.

"I got three offers," he said.

"That's brilliant," I told him. "Which one are you taking?"

His grin faded a bit. "I don't know. That's the problem."

I stopped cutting and looked at him in the mirror. "Mate, that's not a problem. That's the best position you could possibly be in."

He didn't look convinced. "But what if I pick the wrong one?"

"What if you do?" I said. "You'll learn something. You'll figure out what you don't like. And then you'll make a better choice next time. But right now, you get to *choose*. Do you know how rare that is?"

He thought about it. "I guess most of my mates just took the first thing that came along."

"Exactly. And how's that working out for them?"

He laughed. "Not great. Half of them have already quit."

"Right. Because they didn't choose,they just accepted. But you? You've got options. And options change everything."

That conversation stuck with me because it highlighted something most people don't understand: **Having options isn't just about getting a job. It's about learning who you are and what you want.**

When you've only got one offer, you can't learn anything about yourself. You just take it and hope for the best. But when you've got multiple offers, you're forced to ask real questions: What matters to me? What am I willing to compromise on? What's non-negotiable?

Those questions,and the answers you discover,are what set you up for a satisfying life.

Why Options Matter More Than You Think

Let me tell you what happened with Tyler.

He had three offers on the table:

Job 1: A warehouse position. £10.50 an hour, full-time, 20-minute commute. Straightforward work, decent pay, but pretty repetitive.

Job 2: A retail job in town. £9.80 an hour, part-time with potential for full-time, 45-minute commute by bus. More customer interaction, more varied work, but less money and longer travel.

Job 3: An admin role at a small logistics company. £9.50 an hour, full-time, 30-minute commute. Office environment, potential for training and progression, but the lowest starting pay.

If Tyler had only received one of those offers, he would've taken it without thinking. But because he had all three, he had to actually think about what mattered to him.

So I asked him: "What do you care about most right now? Money? Location? The type of work? Growth potential?"

He thought for a minute. "Honestly? I want to learn something. I don't want to be stuck doing the same thing forever."

"Okay," I said. "So which job gives you the best chance to learn?"

He looked at the offers again. "Probably the admin one. They mentioned training. And it's a small company, so I'd probably get to do different things."

"And you're okay with paying the least?"

He nodded. "Yeah. I still live at home. I don't need loads of money right now. I'd rather invest in learning stuff that'll help me later."

That's the power of options. Tyler didn't just pick a job, he made a *strategic decision* based on his priorities. And because he chose it deliberately, he owned it. Six months later, he was still there, learning logistics software, getting involved in different parts of the business, and genuinely enjoying it.

Meanwhile, his mate who took the first warehouse job that came along? Quit after two months because he was bored out of his mind.

Same starting point. Different outcomes. The difference? Tyler had options, and his mate didn't.

The VEM Options Matrix

Here's how I teach young people to think about options. I call it the **VEM Options Matrix**, and it's dead simple.

You take every offer you've got, or even every opportunity you're seriously considering, and you rate it on four factors:

1. **Pay** – How much does it pay? Is that enough for your needs right now?

2. **Location** – How far is it? How easy is the commute? Does that fit your life?

3. **Growth** – Will you learn new skills? Is there room to progress? Or is it a dead-end?

4. **Culture** – Do you like the people? Does the environment feel right? Can you see yourself there?

You don't need a fancy spreadsheet. Just write it down. Give each factor a score out of 10, or rank them high/medium/low. The point isn't to find the "perfect" job, there's no such thing. The point is to see your options clearly and figure out what trade-offs you're willing to make.

Let me show you how this works with a real example.

A lad named Leah had two offers. One was a café job paying £9.20 an hour, 10-minute walk from her house, friendly team, but no real progression. The other was a receptionist role paying £10 an hour, 40-minute commute, more formal environment, but with potential to move into office management.

She was torn. The café felt comfortable and easy. The receptionist role felt like more of a risk.

So we mapped it out:

Café Job:

- Pay: 6/10 (decent but not great)

- Location: 10/10 (walking distance)

- Growth: 3/10 (probably staying a barista)

- Culture: 9/10 (loved the team)

Receptionist Job:

- Pay: 7/10 (better, but not life-changing)

- Location: 5/10 (long commute)

- Growth: 9/10 (clear progression path)

- Culture: 6/10 (seemed fine, but more corporate)

Once she saw it written down, the decision became clearer. She asked herself: "What do I care about most right now?"

And she realized: She was tired of jobs that went nowhere. She wanted to build toward something. So even though the café felt safer, she took the receptionist role.

Three months later, she told me, "I'm so glad I didn't take the easy option. The commute sucks, but I'm learning so much. And they've already started training me on scheduling and invoicing. I actually feel like I'm building a career, not just earning a paycheck."

That's what the Options Matrix does. It doesn't tell you what to choose, it helps you see what *you* value, so you can choose for yourself.

VEM Options Matrix - Rate your job options across four key factors

Options Teach You About Yourself

Here's the thing most people miss: **The value of options isn't just in picking the best one. It's in learning what "best" means to you.**

When you're sixteen, seventeen, eighteen, you probably don't know what you want yet. And that's fine. You're not supposed to.

But you'll never figure it out by sitting around thinking about it. You figure it out by trying things, comparing them, and noticing what feels right and what doesn't.

That's why volume is so important. The more applications you send, the more options you create. The more options you have, the more you're forced to evaluate and compare. And the more you evaluate and compare, the clearer your priorities become.

Let me give you an example.

A lad named Ethan came to me with no idea what he wanted to do. "I just need a job," he said. "I don't care what it is."

I told him, "Okay, but let's create some options so you can figure out what you *do* care about."

He sent applications everywhere. Retail, hospitality, warehouses, call centers, admin roles. Within a month, he had five interviews lined up.

After the first interview,at a call center,he came back and said, "I don't think I want to do that. It felt really scripted. Like I wouldn't be able to just talk to people normally."

Okay. So now he knew he didn't like overly structured environments.

After the second interview,at a sports shop,he said, "That was better. I liked that I could actually chat with customers about stuff I know about."

Okay. So he liked customer interaction and using his interests.

After the third interview,at a warehouse,he said, "That felt too isolated. I don't want to just be moving boxes all day with no one to talk to."

Okay. So he valued social interaction.

By the time he'd done all five interviews, he had a pretty clear picture: He wanted a job where he could talk to people, use his interests, and not feel like a robot following a script.

He ended up taking a job at a bike shop. Not the highest-paying offer, but the best fit for what he'd learned about himself.

And here's the key: **He only learned that by having options.** If he'd just taken the first job that came along, he might've ended up in that call center, hating every minute, thinking "I guess I'm just not a work person."

But he's not "not a work person." He just needed to find work that fit him. And the only way to do that was to create options and compare them.

The Long-Term Impact of Learning to Choose

This isn't just about getting your first job. This is about building a skill that'll serve you for the rest of your life.

Think about it. Over the next fifty years, you're going to make thousands of decisions. What job to take? Whether to go to university. What to study. Where to live. Who to live with. Whether to stay in a relationship or leave. Whether to take a risk or play it safe.

Every single one of those decisions will be easier if you've practiced making decisions.

And you practice by having options.

When you're used to evaluating multiple job offers, you get better at evaluating university courses. When you're used to weighing trade-offs,pay vs location, growth vs comfort,you get better at weighing trade-offs in every area of life.

The young people I work with who've gone through the VEM process don't just get jobs faster. They make better decisions. They're more confident. They know what they want. They don't just drift through life accepting whatever comes, they actively shape their lives.

And it all starts with creating options.

What This Means for You

If you want to unlock the power of options, here's what to do:

Step 1: Create volume. You can't have options if you're not applying widely. Ten applications per week. That's the baseline. More is better.

Step 2: Track your options. When you get interview requests or offers, write them down. Don't just keep them in your head. Seeing them on paper (or on a screen) makes them real and helps you compare.

Step 3: Use the VEM Options Matrix. For every opportunity, rate it on Pay, Location, Growth, and Culture. You don't need to be scientific about it, just honest. What matters to you? What are you willing to compromise on?

Step 4: Make a decision. Don't overthink it. You're not looking for perfection, you're looking for the best fit based on what you know right now. Pick one and commit.

Step 5: Reflect. After a few weeks or months, ask yourself: Did I make the right choice? What did I learn? What would I do differently next time? This reflection is how you get better at decision-making over time.

For teens: Having options isn't about being greedy or indecisive. It's about giving yourself the power to choose. Don't feel guilty for comparing offers or asking for time to think. This is *your* life. You get to decide what fits.

For parents: When your teen has multiple offers, resist the urge to tell them which one to pick. Instead, help them think through their priorities. Ask: "What matters most to you right now?" "What are you willing to compromise on?" "What would you regret not trying?" Your job is to guide the process, not make the decision.

For educators: Teach students that options are a *good* thing, not a source of stress. Build decision-making frameworks into your careers program. Show them how to evaluate opportunities. Give them practice comparing hypothetical offers. The skill of choosing well is just as important as the skill of applying well.

Options aren't a luxury. They're a necessity.

Because when you don't have options, you don't have control. You're just accepting whatever life hands you and hoping it works out.

But when you create options,when you apply widely, generate multiple opportunities, and learn to evaluate them,you take control. You become the driver, not the passenger.

And that changes everything.

Chapter Six

PRACTICING DECISIONS

Becoming a Good Chooser, Not Just a Lucky One

I 'll never forget the day Jordan came into the shop looking absolutely gutted.

"I made the wrong choice," he said.

He'd had two job offers a few months earlier. One was a retail job at a big chain store,stable, predictable, decent pay. The other was at a small independent shop,less pay, less security, but the owner had promised to teach him about running a business.

He'd picked the independent shop. And now, three months in, the shop was struggling. Hours were getting cut. The owner was stressed and had stopped doing any training. Jordan felt like he'd made a huge mistake.

"I should've taken the safe option," he said. "I'm an idiot."

I put down my clippers. "Mate, you're not an idiot. You made a decision based on what you knew at the time. And now you've learned something."

"Yeah," he said bitterly. "I learned I'm bad at making decisions."

"No," I said. "You learned that small businesses can be risky. You learned that promises about training don't always pan out. You learned that stability matters more to you than you thought. That's not failure. That's data."

He looked at me like I was trying to make him feel better with nonsense.

"I'm serious," I said. "You think people who make good decisions just magically know the right answer every time? They don't. They've just practiced making decisions, learning from them, and getting better over time. You're not bad at decisions,you're just early in the process."

That conversation changed how I think about decision-making. Because here's the truth: **Nobody is naturally good at making decisions. It's a skill you build through practice.**

And the only way to practice is to make decisions, see what happens, and adjust.

The Myth of the "Right" Decision

We've been taught to believe that for every situation, there's one right decision and a bunch of wrong ones. And if you're smart enough, careful enough, thoughtful enough, you'll figure out which one is right.

That's rubbish.

Most decisions don't have a "right" answer. They have trade-offs. You pick the option that aligns best with your priorities at that moment, and then you deal with the consequences,good and bad.

Jordan didn't make the "wrong" decision when he picked the independent shop. He made a reasonable decision based on his priorities at the time. He valued learning over stability. That's not wrong,it's just a choice.

What he learned from that choice was that his priorities were different than he thought. He discovered that he actually valued stability more than he'd realized. And that's incredibly valuable information.

Now, when he makes his next decision, he'll be better equipped. He'll know to ask more questions about financial stability. He'll know to get training promises in writing. He'll know that his risk tolerance isn't as high as he thought.

That's not failure. That's growth.

But here's the problem: Most people don't see it that way. They make one decision that doesn't work out perfectly, and they conclude they're bad at decisions. So they stop making them. They let other people decide for them. They drift. And then they wonder why their life doesn't feel like theirs.

How to Become a Good Chooser

So how do you get good at making decisions?

The same way you get good at anything: **practice, feedback, adjustment, repeat.**

Let me break that down.

Step 1: Practice. You have to actually make decisions. Not hypothetical ones, real ones with real consequences. That's why creating options through volume is so important. You can't practice decision-making if you don't have decisions to make.

Step 2: Feedback. After you make a decision, pay attention to what happens. Not just whether it "worked" or "didn't work," but *why*. What did you learn? What surprised you? What would you do differently?

Step 3: Adjustment. Use what you learned to inform your next decision. Maybe you learned you value flexibility more than pay. Maybe you learned you hate long commutes. Maybe you learned you need a structured environment to thrive. Whatever it is, take it with you.

Step 4: Repeat. Make another decision. And another. And another. Each time, you'll get a little better at predicting what you'll like, what you'll regret, and what trade-offs you're willing to make.

This is how you become a good chooser. Not by magically knowing the right answer, but by building a track record of decisions, learning from them, and refining your process.

Let me show you what this looks like in practice.

The Story of Mia: Learning to Choose

Mia was seventeen when I first met her. She used to bring her little brother in for a haircut. She'd just finished college and had no idea what she wanted to do. So we started with volume, ten applications a week, a wide range of industries, just to see what stuck.

Within a month, she had three offers:

1. A receptionist job at a dental practice.

2. A sales assistant role at a clothing shop.

3. An admin position at a logistics company.

She picked the clothing shop. Why? "I like fashion, and I thought it'd be fun." Fair enough.

Two months later, she came back. "I hate it," she said. "It's so boring. We just fold clothes and deal with returns all day. I thought it'd be more creative, but it's just retail."

"Okay," I said. "What did you learn?"

She thought about it. "I learned that liking something as a hobby doesn't mean I'll like it as a job. And I learned I don't like standing around all day. I want to be doing something."

"Good," I said. "So what's next?"

She started applying again. This time, she avoided retail. She focused on roles that involved more variety, admin, coordination, customer service.

She got two more offers:

1. A customer service role at a call center.

2. An admin assistant job at a marketing agency.

She picked the marketing agency. Why? "I want to see what marketing's like. And the job description said I'd be helping with events and social media, which sounds more interesting than just answering phones."

Three months later, she came back with a completely different energy.

"I love it," she said. "I'm learning so much. I'm helping organize events, I'm managing their Instagram, I'm doing a bit of everything. It's exactly what I wanted."

"So what did you learn this time?" I asked.

"I learned I like variety. I like being involved in different things. I like creative work, but I also like the organizational side. And I learned that I'm actually pretty good at this."

That's the process. Mia didn't magically find the perfect job on her first try. She made a decision, learned from it, adjusted, and made a better decision next time.

And now? She's not just in a job she likes, she's learned what kind of work suits her. She knows she values variety, creativity, and being involved in multiple projects. That knowledge will guide every decision she makes for the rest of her career.

That's what practicing decisions does. It teaches you about yourself.

The "Wrong" Choice Is Still a Useful Choice

Here's something I wish more people understood: **Even the "wrong" choice teaches you something valuable.**

Jordan learned that he values stability more than he thought. Mia learned that liking fashion doesn't mean she'll like working in a clothing shop. Both of those lessons came from choices that didn't work out the way they hoped.

But those weren't wasted experiences. They were *essential* experiences. Because now Jordan and Mia know themselves better. They've refined their priorities. They've learned what to look for and what to avoid.

You can't learn that by thinking. You can only learn it by doing.

And here's the thing: The earlier you make these "mistakes," the better. Because the cost of a bad decision at seventeen is way lower than the cost of a bad decision at thirty-five.

If you pick the wrong job at seventeen, you quit and try something else. No big deal.

If you pick the wrong career at thirty-five because you never practiced making decisions, you're stuck. You've got a mortgage, kids, responsibilities. You can't just walk away.

That's why I tell young people: **Make your mistakes now. Try things. Get it wrong. Learn from it. Build the skill of decision-making while the stakes are still low.**

Because the stakes won't stay low forever.

How to Evaluate Your Decisions

Alright, practical stuff. When you make a decision,whether it's which job to take, which course to study, or which opportunity to pursue,here's how to evaluate it afterward:

1. What did I expect to happen? Write down what you thought the job/course/opportunity would be like before you started. Be specific.

2. What actually happened? After a few weeks or months, write down what it's actually like. Where did reality match your expectations? Where did it differ?

3. What did I learn about the opportunity? What surprised you? What was better than expected? What was worse?

4. What did I learn about myself? What did this experience teach you about your preferences, priorities, strengths, and weaknesses?

5. What will I do differently next time? Based on what you learned, how will you approach your next decision? What questions will you ask? What factors will you prioritize?

This reflection process is how you turn experience into wisdom. Without it, you're just bouncing from one thing to the next without learning anything.

With it, every decision,good or bad,makes you better at the next one.

What This Means for You

If you want to become a good chooser, here's what to do:

For teens:

Stop waiting for the perfect decision. There isn't one. Make a choice based on what you know now, commit to it, and see what happens. If it works out, great. If it doesn't, you've learned something. Either way, you're building the skill.

Keep a decision journal. Every time you make a significant choice, write down why you made it and what you expected. Then, a few months later, write down what actually happened and what you learned. Over time, you'll see patterns in your preferences and priorities.

Don't beat yourself up for "wrong" choices. Every choice teaches you something. The only real mistake is not learning from it.

For parents:

When your teen makes a decision that doesn't work out, resist the urge to say "I told you so" or "You should have listened to me." Instead, ask: "What did you learn?" Help them extract the lesson, not the shame.

Encourage your teen to make decisions while they're still living at home and the stakes are low. Let them try things, fail, and try again. That's how they build the skill.

Model good decision-making yourself. Talk through your own choices out loud,why you're considering different options, what trade-offs you're weighing, how you'll evaluate the outcome. Let them see that decision-making is a process, not a moment of inspiration.

For educators:

Teach decision-making as a skill, not a personality trait. Show students the process: create options, evaluate trade-offs, make a choice, reflect, adjust.

Use real examples. Bring in recent graduates to talk about decisions they made, what worked, what didn't, and what they learned. Show students that "wrong" choices are part of the process.

Build reflection into your careers program. After students do work experience or apply for jobs, have them write about what they learned,not just about the job, but about themselves.

Becoming a good chooser isn't about always making the right decision. It's about making decisions, learning from them, and getting better over time.

And the only way to do that is to practice.

So stop overthinking. Stop waiting for certainty. Stop being afraid of getting it wrong.

Make a choice. See what happens. Learn from it. Make another choice. That's how you build a life you actually want, one decision at a time.

Chapter Seven

PARENT PARTNERSHIP

Helping Without Taking the Wheel

T he mum sat down in the chair next to her son, pulled out her phone, and said, "Right, let's go through your CV while Errol's cutting your hair."

The lad, sixteen, maybe seventeen, looked mortified.

I caught his eye in the mirror and gave him a sympathetic look. Then I turned to the mum and said, as gently as I could, "You know what? I bet he's got this. Why don't you let him tell me about his job search, and you can just relax for a bit?"

She looked at me like I'd suggested she jump out of a plane. "But he won't do it properly if I don't help."

"Maybe," I said. "Or maybe he'll surprise you."

She reluctantly put her phone away, and I started chatting with the lad. Turns out, he'd already sent five applications that week, had an interview lined up, and had a pretty clear idea of what he was looking for.

His mum had no idea. Because she'd been so busy trying to manage the process that she hadn't actually asked him what he was doing.

After they left, I thought about that interaction for days. Because I see it all the time: **Parents who love their kids so much that they accidentally take over their lives.**

And I get it. I really do. You want your kid to succeed. You don't want them to struggle or make mistakes or miss opportunities. You've got experience they don't have, and you want to share it.

But here's the hard truth: **When you take the wheel, you rob them of the chance to learn how to drive.**

The Support vs Takeover Line

There's a fine line between supporting your teen and taking over. And most parents don't realize when they've crossed it.

Support looks like:

- "How's the job search going?"

- "Do you want to talk through your options?"

- "I'm here if you need help."

Takeover looks like:

- "I've rewritten your CV for you."

- "I've found three jobs you should apply for."

- "Let me call them and ask why you didn't get the interview."

The difference? **Support empowers. Takeover disempowers.**

When you support your teen, you're giving them tools, encouragement, and a safety net. You're helping them build confidence and skills.

When you take over, you're sending a message: "I don't trust you to do this on your own." And even if that's not what you mean, that's what they hear.

Let me tell you about a dad named Richard.

His son, Ben, was eighteen and looking for work. Richard was a successful manager at a logistics company, and he was convinced he knew exactly how Ben should approach the job search.

He rewrote Ben's CV. He told Ben which jobs to apply for. He even called a few companies on Ben's behalf to "put in a good word."

And Ben? Ben stopped trying.

He'd send an application here and there, but his heart wasn't in it. He'd go to interviews, but he seemed defeated before he even started.

Richard came to me, frustrated. "I'm doing everything I can to help him, and he's just not putting in the effort."

I asked him, "Have you asked Ben what he wants?"

Richard looked confused. "What do you mean?"

"I mean, what does *Ben* want? What kind of work is he interested in? What are his priorities? Have you actually asked him, or have you just been telling him what to do?"

Richard went quiet.

The next week, he came back. "I talked to Ben," he said. "Really talked to him. Turns out, he doesn't want to work in an office. He wants to do something hands-on. And he's been feeling like I don't think he's capable of figuring this out on his own."

"What did you say?" I asked.

"I told him I'm sorry. I told him I trust him. And I asked him how I can actually help instead of just taking over."

Two weeks later, Ben came in for a trim. Different energy entirely. He'd applied for apprenticeships in carpentry and plumbing,things he was actually interested in. He had an interview coming up. He was excited.

"What changed?" I asked.

"My dad backed off," he said. "And I realized I actually want to do this. I just didn't want to do it *his* way."

That's the power of stepping back. When you give your teen space to own their process, they step up.

How to Be a Supportive Parent (Without Taking Over)

Scripts for Support, Not Takeover

Alright, practical stuff. If you're a parent and you want to help without taking over, here are some phrases that work:

Instead of: "You need to apply for this job." **Try:** "I saw this job posting. Do you think it's something you'd be interested in?"

Instead of: "Your CV is wrong. Let me fix it." **Try:** "Would you like me to look over your CV and give you some feedback?"

Instead of: "Why haven't you heard back yet? I'm going to call them." **Try:** "I know waiting is hard. How are you feeling about it?"

Instead of: "You should take the job with better pay." **Try:** "What matters most to you,pay, location, or growth potential?"

Instead of: "You're not trying hard enough." **Try:** "What's one thing you could do this week to move forward?"

See the difference? The first set of phrases takes control. The second set invites collaboration.

Your teen doesn't need you to do it for them. They need you to believe they *can* do it.

The Story of Sarah: A Mum Who Learned to Let Go

Sarah's daughter, Chloe, was seventeen and struggling to find work. Sarah was worried. She'd seen too many of Chloe's friends drift into dead-end jobs or give up entirely, and she didn't want that for her daughter.

So Sarah started managing the process. She'd check Chloe's application tracker every day. She'd remind her to follow up. She'd critique every CV draft. She meant well, but Chloe was getting more and more frustrated.

One day, Chloe snapped. "Mum, I can't do this with you hovering over me all the time. I need to figure this out on my own."

Sarah was hurt. She came to me and said, "I'm just trying to help. Why is she pushing me away?"

I asked her, "If you were learning to drive and someone kept grabbing the wheel every time you made a mistake, how would you feel?"

She thought about it. "I'd feel like they didn't trust me."

"Exactly."

Sarah decided to try something different. She told Chloe, "I'm sorry for taking over. I trust you to handle this. But I'm here if you need me."

And then she stepped back.

It was hard. She wanted to check in every day. She wanted to remind Chloe to apply. She wanted to make sure things were moving forward.

But she didn't. She waited for Chloe to come to her.

And eventually, Chloe did.

"Mum, can you help me practice for an interview?" she asked one day.

Sarah was thrilled. Not because she got to be involved, but because Chloe had *asked*. She wasn't taking over, she was being invited in.

They practiced together. Chloe got the job. And Sarah learned that her daughter was more capable than she'd given her credit for.

"I realized," Sarah told me later, "that my job isn't to make sure she succeeds. It's to make sure she knows I believe she can."

That's the shift every parent needs to make.

What Teens Actually Need from Parents

I've asked hundreds of young people what they need from their parents during the job search. Here's what they say:

1. Belief. "I need my parents to believe I can do this, even when I don't believe it myself."

2. Space. "I need room to try, fail, and figure it out without them jumping in to fix everything."

3. Encouragement. "I need them to celebrate the small wins, like sending an application or getting an interview, not just the final outcome."

4. Perspective. "I need them to remind me that rejection isn't the end of the world, and that everyone goes through this."

5. Practical help, when asked. "I need them to be available when I ask for help, but not to force help on me when I don't."

Notice what's not on that list? "I need my parents to do it for me."

Your teen doesn't want you to take over. They want you to be their safety net, not their driver.

When to Step In (and When to Step Back)

Okay, so when *should* you get involved?

Step in when:

- Your teen asks for help.

- Your teen is genuinely stuck and has tried multiple approaches without success.

- Your teen is being treated unfairly or unsafely (e.g., an employer asking inappropriate questions, unsafe working conditions).

Step back when:

- Your teen is making progress, even if it's slower than you'd like.

- Your teen is learning from mistakes.

- Your teen hasn't asked for your input.

And here's the key: **Even when you step in, don't take over.** Offer guidance, not solutions. Ask questions, don't give orders.

For example:

Instead of: "Here's what you should do." **Try:** "What do you think your options are?"

Instead of: "Let me handle this." **Try:** "How can I support you with this?"

Your job is to coach, not to play the game for them.

What This Means for You

For parents:

Check yourself. Are you supporting or taking over? If you're not sure, ask your teen. Say, "Am I helping, or am I being too much?" And then actually listen to their answer.

Focus on effort, not outcomes. Celebrate when your teen sends applications, practices interviews, or reflects on what they've learned,not just when they get a job.

Let them own their decisions. Even if you think they're making the wrong choice, let them make it (unless it's genuinely dangerous). They'll learn more from a "wrong" choice they made themselves than from a "right" choice you made for them.

Be the safety net, not the helicopter. Your job is to catch them if they fall, not to prevent them from ever falling.

For teens:

If your parents are taking over, talk to them. Say, "I know you're trying to help, but I need to do this myself. Can you support me without managing me?" Most parents will respect that if you say it clearly and calmly.

Ask for help when you need it. Don't shut your parents out completely. They've got experience and perspective that can be valuable, just make sure you're inviting them in, not letting them take over.

For educators:

Help parents understand the line between support and takeover. Offer workshops or resources on how to empower teens without controlling them.

Encourage parents to focus on the process, not just the outcome. Share data showing that resilience and decision-making skills matter more than landing the perfect first job.

The goal isn't to get parents out of the picture. It's to get them in the *right* part of the picture.

Your teen needs you. But they need you as a partner, not a manager.

So step back. Trust them. Believe in them.

And watch them surprise you.

Chapter Eight

FROM NO TO KNOW
Turning Rejection Into Data

T he text came through at 4:47 PM on a Thursday.

"Didn't get it. I'm done."

It was from a lad named Callum. Eighteen years old, I had been applying for jobs for about a month. This was his third rejection in two weeks, and he was ready to give up.

I called him. "What happened?"

"They said I didn't have enough experience. Same thing everyone says. I can't get experience if no one will hire me, so what's the point?"

"Did they say anything else?" I asked.

"Not really. Just a generic email. 'Thank you for your interest, we've decided to move forward with other candidates.' The usual."

"Okay," I said. "So what did you learn?"

He was quiet for a second. "What do you mean, what did I learn? I learned I'm not good enough."

"No," I said. "That's not what you learned. You learned that *this particular employer* wanted someone with more experience. That's not about you being good enough. That's about fit. So what are you going to do with that information?"

Another pause. "I don't know."

"Alright," I said. "Here's what we're going to do. Every time you get a rejection, we're going to treat it like data. Not like a judgment. Data. And we're going to use that data to get better. Sounds good?"

He didn't sound convinced, but he agreed.

Three months later, Callum had a job. And when I asked him what made the difference, he said, "I stopped taking rejection personally. I started asking, 'What can I learn from this?' And once I did that, everything changed."

That's what this chapter is about: **Turning rejection from something that defeats you into something that teaches you.**

Why Rejection Feels Personal (Even Though It Isn't)

Let's be honest: Rejection sucks.

It doesn't matter how many times someone tells you "it's not personal" or "it's just part of the process." When you get that email or that phone call saying "no," it feels personal.

And there's a reason for that. Our brains are wired to interpret rejection as a threat. Back when we lived in small tribes, being rejected by the group could literally mean death. So our brains learned to treat rejection as dangerous.

That's why it hurts. That's why it makes you want to give up. Your brain is trying to protect you by saying, "Stop putting yourself out there. It's not safe."

But here's the thing: **Your brain is wrong.**

Rejection in the modern world,especially job rejection,isn't dangerous. It's just information. It's feedback. It's data.

The problem is, most people don't treat it that way. They treat it like a verdict on their worth. And when you do that, every "no" becomes evidence that you're not good enough.

But what if you flipped the script? What if every "no" became evidence that you're learning, adapting, and getting closer to a "yes"?

That's the shift I teach. And it changes everything.

The Three Types of Rejection (and What to Learn from Each)

Not all rejections are the same. And once you understand the different types, you can extract different lessons from each one.

Type 1: The Silent Rejection

This is when you apply and never hear back. No email, no phone call, nothing.

It's frustrating, but here's what it usually means: Your application didn't make it past the first filter. Maybe the job description asked for specific qualifications you didn't mention. Maybe your CV wasn't formatted in a way that was easy to scan. Maybe they got 200 applications and yours just didn't stand out.

What to learn: Your application needs to be clearer and more targeted. Look at the job description again. Did you use the same keywords they used? Did you make it obvious that you meet their requirements? If not, adjust.

Type 2: The Generic Rejection

This is the "thank you for your interest, but we've decided to move forward with other candidates" email.

It's vague, and it doesn't give you much to work with. But here's what it usually means: You were in the running, but someone else was a better fit. Maybe they had more experience. Maybe they had a specific skill the employer needed. Maybe they just clicked better in the interview.

What to learn: You're doing something right,you're getting past the first filter. But you need to find ways to stand out more. Maybe that's gaining a specific skill. Maybe that's improving your interview technique. Maybe that's applying to roles that are a better fit for your current experience level.

Type 3: The Specific Rejection

This is when an employer actually tells you *why* you didn't get the job. "We were looking for someone with more experience in X." "We felt your communication skills weren't quite at the level we needed." "We decided to go with an internal candidate."

This is the most valuable type of rejection, because it gives you something concrete to work on.

What to learn: Take the feedback seriously. If they said you need more experience, find ways to get it,volunteer work, short-term projects, online courses. If they said your communication needs work, practice. If they went with an internal candidate, that's not about you at all,just bad timing.

The Story of Aisha: Harvesting Lessons from Rejection

Let me tell you about Aisha.

She was nineteen, she used to bring her nephew in for a haircut, she had been applying for jobs for two months, and had been rejected from twelve positions. She was ready to quit.

"I'm obviously doing something wrong," she said. "But I don't know what."

So I asked her to bring me every rejection she'd received. We went through them one by one.

Rejection 1-4: No response at all.

Lesson: Her CV wasn't getting past the initial filter. We looked at the job descriptions and realized she wasn't using the right keywords. She was describing her skills in her own words, but employers were scanning for specific terms. We adjusted her CV to mirror the language in the job postings.

Rejection 5-8: Generic "we've moved forward with other candidates" emails.

Lesson: She was getting noticed, but not standing out. We worked on her cover letters, making them more specific to each role. Instead of "I'm a hard worker," she wrote, "In my volunteer role at the community center, I managed a schedule for 15 volunteers and organized three events, which taught me how to coordinate multiple tasks under pressure."

Rejection 9-10: She got to the interview stage but didn't get the job.

Lesson: Her interview skills needed work. We did mock interviews, and I recorded her on my phone so she could watch herself back. She realized she was giving one-word answers and not making eye contact. We practiced until she felt more confident.

Rejection 11-12: She got to the final round but lost out to someone with more experience.

Lesson: She was doing everything right, she just needed to keep going. The competition was tough, but she was close.

By the time she got to application number fifteen, she'd incorporated all those lessons. And she got the job.

"I can't believe it," she said. "I was so close to giving up."

"But you didn't," I said. "You treated every 'no' like data. And that's what made the difference."

How to Analyze Your Rejections

Alright, here's a practical system for turning rejection into learning.

Step 1: Track every application. Keep a simple spreadsheet or document with the job title, company, date applied, and outcome. This gives you a clear picture of your progress.

Step 2: Categorize your rejections. Silent, generic, or specific? Knowing which type you're getting most often tells you where to focus.

Step 3: Look for patterns. Are you getting rejected at the same stage every time? Are certain types of jobs more responsive than others? Patterns reveal what's working and what's not.

Step 4: Ask for feedback. If you get a generic rejection, reply and politely ask if they can share any feedback. Most won't respond, but some will, and that information is gold.

Step 5: Adjust and try again. Use what you've learned to improve your next application. Then send it. Don't wait until everything's perfect, just make it better than last time.

Reframing Rejection: It's Not About You

Here's the mindset shift that changes everything: **Rejection isn't about your worth. It's about fit.**

When an employer says no, they're not saying you're a bad person or that you'll never succeed. They're saying, "This particular role, at this particular company, at this particular time, isn't the right fit."

That's it.

Maybe they needed someone with a specific skill you don't have yet. Maybe they had an internal candidate they were always going to choose. Maybe they got 150 applications and could only interview five. Maybe the hiring manager's cousin applied and they felt obligated.

None of that is about you.

But when you take it personally, you make it about you. And that's when rejection becomes paralyzing.

So here's what I tell every young person I work with: **Every "no" is just clearing the path to your "yes."**

You don't want a job where you're not the right fit. You don't want to work for an employer who doesn't see your value. Every rejection is just eliminating an option that wasn't going to work out anyway.

And every rejection is training. It's practice. It's one more rep that makes you better, stronger, and more resilient.

What This Means for You

For teens:

Stop treating rejection like failure. It's not. It's feedback. Every "no" teaches you something,about the job market, about what employers want, about how to present yourself better.

Keep a rejection journal. Write down every rejection and what you learned from it. Over time, you'll see that you're not stuck,you're improving.

Remember: You only need one "yes." It doesn't matter if you get fifty "nos" along the way. The only one that counts is the one that works out.

For parents:

When your teen gets rejected, don't try to fix it or make them feel better with empty reassurances. Instead, ask: "What do you think you can learn from this?" Help them see rejection as data, not defeat.

Share your own rejection stories. Let them know that everyone,including you,has been told "no" many times. Normalize it.

Celebrate effort, not just outcomes. When your teen sends an application or goes to an interview, that's worth celebrating, even if it doesn't lead to a job.

For educators:

Teach students that rejection is part of the process, not a sign of failure. Build resilience by normalizing rejection and showing them how to learn from it.

Bring in guest speakers who can share their rejection stories,and how those rejections led to better opportunities.

Create a "rejection wall" where students can anonymously post their rejections and what they learned. Show them they're not alone.

Rejection isn't the end. It's just information.

And when you learn to treat it that way, it loses its power over you.

So the next time you get a "no," don't spiral. Don't give up. Don't take it personally.

Just ask: "What can I learn from this?"

And then use that knowledge to get better.

Because every "no" is training for your eventual "yes."

Chapter Nine

THE CONFIDENCE CURVE

Bandura, Barber Chairs, and the Science of Doing

There's a moment every barber knows.

It's when you hand a new apprentice the clippers for the first time and watch them freeze. They've watched you do a hundred fades. They've practiced on mannequin heads. They know the theory.

But now there's a real person in the chair, and their hands are shaking.

"I can't do this," they say.

And I always say the same thing: "You can't do it *yet*. But you will. You just need reps."

Because here's the truth: **Confidence doesn't come from feeling ready. It comes from doing the thing over and over until you realize you can.**

That's not just barber shop wisdom. That's science.

A psychologist named Albert Bandura spent his entire career studying how people build confidence,or, as he called it, *self-efficacy*. And what he found was simple but powerful: **The most effective way to build confidence is through mastery experiences.**

Not positive thinking. Not visualization. Not affirmations.

Doing.

You build confidence by doing the thing, getting feedback, adjusting, and doing it again. Over and over. Until one day, you realize you're not scared anymore. You're just competent.

That's the confidence curve. And understanding it changes everything.

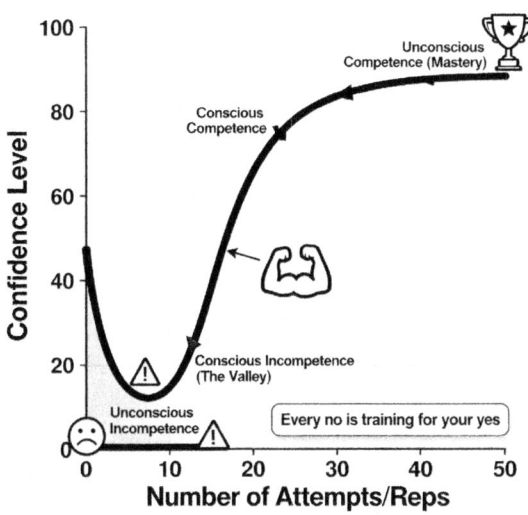

The Confidence Curve - Four stages from incompetence to mastery

The Four Stages of the Confidence Curve

When you're learning something new,whether it's cutting hair, applying for jobs, or making decisions,you go through four predictable stages.

Stage 1: Unconscious Incompetence (You Don't Know What You Don't Know)

This is the very beginning. You're excited, maybe a bit naive. You think, "How hard can it be?"

In the job search, this is when you send your first application and assume you'll hear back in a few days. You don't yet know how competitive it is, how many applications employers get, or how long the process takes.

You're not confident, but you're not worried either. You just don't know enough to be worried.

Stage 2: Conscious Incompetence (You Know You Don't Know)

This is the hard part. You've sent a few applications and gotten nothing back. Or you've done an interview and it went badly. Suddenly, you realize: *This is harder than I thought.*

This is where most people quit.

Because now you're aware of how much you don't know, and it's overwhelming. You feel incompetent, and you're painfully conscious of it.

In the barber shop, this is when the apprentice has done five bad haircuts and is convinced they'll never get it right.

In the job search, this is when you've been rejected ten times and you're thinking, "Maybe I'm just not cut out for this."

This stage sucks. But it's also the most important one. Because this is where growth happens.

Stage 3: Conscious Competence (You Know, But You Have to Think About It)

This is when things start to click. You're getting better, but it still takes effort. You have to think about every step. You're not smooth yet, but you're functional.

In the barber shop, this is when the apprentice can do a decent fade, but they're concentrating hard the whole time, checking and rechecking every line.

In the job search, this is when you've figured out how to write a decent CV, you know what to say in interviews, and you're starting to get responses. It's still nerve-wracking, but you're seeing progress.

Stage 4: Unconscious Competence (You Just Do It)

This is mastery. You don't have to think about it anymore. It's automatic. You're confident because you've done it so many times that it's second nature.

In the barber shop, this is when the apprentice can chat with the customer, listen to music, and still deliver a perfect fade without breaking a sweat.

In the job search, this is when you can send applications without agonizing over every word, walk into interviews feeling calm, and evaluate offers with clarity.

You're not confident because you're naturally talented. You're confident because you've done the reps.

Why Most People Quit at Stage 2

Here's the problem: Stage 2, conscious incompetence,feels terrible.

You're aware of how much you don't know. You're making mistakes. You're getting rejected. And your brain is screaming at you to stop.

This is where people say, "I'm just not good at this" or "This isn't for me" or "I'll never figure it out."

But here's the truth: **Everyone goes through Stage 2. Everyone.**

The people who succeed aren't more talented or naturally confident. They just push through Stage 2 instead of quitting.

Let me tell you about a lad named Dev.

Dev came to me after sending about eight applications and getting zero responses. He was in full Stage 2 mode, painfully aware that he didn't know what he was doing, and convinced he'd never figure it out.

"I think I'm just bad at this," he said.

"You're not bad at it," I told him. "You're just early in the process. You're in the hard part. But if you keep going, it gets easier."

He didn't believe me. But he agreed to try.

We worked on his CV. We practiced his interview technique. He kept sending applications,ten a week, like I'd taught him.

For the first few weeks, nothing changed. He was still getting rejections. He was still in Stage 2.

But then, slowly, things started to shift.

He got an interview request. Then another. Then an offer.

By week eight, he had three offers on the table and was evaluating which one to take.

"I can't believe how different this feels," he said. "A few weeks ago, I was convinced I'd never get a job. Now I'm choosing between three."

"That's the confidence curve," I told him. "You didn't get more talented. You just did the reps. And now you're in Stage 3."

Six months later, Dev came back for a trim. He'd just started looking for a new job, he wanted something with more growth potential, and he told me, "This time, I'm not scared at all. I know how to do this now."

That's Stage 4. Unconscious competence. He'd done it enough times that it didn't feel hard anymore.

Bandura's Four Sources of Self-Efficacy - The science behind confidence building

Bandura's Four Sources of Self-Efficacy

Alright, let's get into the science for a minute.

Albert Bandura identified four ways people build confidence:

1. Mastery Experiences

This is the most powerful source. You do the thing, you succeed (even partially), and you think, "I can do this."

Every application you send, every interview you complete, every rejection you bounce back from,those are mastery experiences. They're building your confidence, even when it doesn't feel like it.

2. Vicarious Experiences

This is when you see someone else do it and think, "If they can, I can."

This is why success stories matter. When you hear about someone who was in your exact position,no experience, lots of rejections,and they made it through, it gives you hope.

That's why I share stories in this book. Not to brag, but to show you: If they did it, you can too.

3. Verbal Persuasion

This is when someone you trust tells you, "You can do this."

It's not as powerful as mastery experiences, but it helps. Especially when you're in Stage 2 and you're doubting yourself.

This is where parents, teachers, and mentors come in. Your job isn't to do it for them, it's to remind them they're capable.

4. Managing Your Emotional State

This is about learning to calm your nerves and stay focused.

If you go into an interview feeling panicked, you won't perform well. But if you've practiced enough that you feel calm, you'll do better.

This is why mock interviews help. They let you practice managing your nerves in a low-stakes environment.

Of these four, mastery experiences are by far the most powerful. Nothing builds confidence like actually doing the thing.

But here's the key:

You need repeated mastery experiences, not just one.

One success could be luck. Ten successes? That's a pattern. That's proof. That's confidence.

The Confidence Curve in Action: A Visual

Imagine a graph. On the horizontal axis, you've got "number of attempts." On the vertical axis, you've got "confidence level."

At the beginning, your confidence is low. You're in Stage 1,

you don't know what you don't know.

Then it drops even lower. You're in Stage 2,

you're painfully aware of your incompetence. This is the valley. This is where most people quit.

But if you keep going, the line starts to climb. Slowly at first, then faster. You're in Stage 3,

you're getting better, and you can feel it.

Eventually, the line levels off at a high point. You're in Stage 4,

you're confident because you've done it so many times that it's automatic.

That curve,the dip and then the climb,is universal. Everyone goes through it.

The only difference between people who succeed and people who quit is whether they push through the valley.

What This Means for You

For teens:

Understand that confidence comes *after* you do the thing, not before. You're not supposed to feel confident when you start. You're supposed to feel nervous, uncertain, maybe even incompetent. That's normal.

Your job is to do the reps anyway. Send the applications. Go to the interviews. Make the mistakes. Learn from them. Keep going.

Every time you do, you're moving along the confidence curve. You're getting closer to Stage 4.

Track your progress. Write down how many applications you've sent, how many interviews you've done, how many offers you've received. Seeing the numbers go up will remind you that you're improving, even when it doesn't feel like it.

For parents:

When your teen is in Stage 2,when they're struggling and doubting themselves,don't try to rescue them. Don't do it for them. Just remind them: "This is the hard part. Everyone goes through this. But if you keep going, it gets easier."

Celebrate the reps, not just the results. Every application sent, every interview completed, every rejection bounced back from,those are wins. Acknowledge them.

Share your own Stage 2 stories. Let them know that you've been in the valley too, and you made it through.

For educators:

Teach students about the confidence curve. Show them the graph. Explain that Stage 2 is normal and temporary.

Build mastery experiences into your program. Give students opportunities to practice,mock interviews, application workshops, feedback sessions. The more reps they do in a safe environment, the more confident they'll be in the real world.

Normalize struggle. Let students know that everyone feels incompetent at first. That's not a sign they're failing,it's a sign they're learning.

Confidence isn't something you're born with. It's something you build.

And you build it the same way you build anything: one rep at a time.

So stop waiting to feel ready. Stop waiting to feel confident.

Just start.

Do the thing. Get feedback. Adjust. Do it again.

And one day, sooner than you think, you'll realize you're not scared anymore.

You're just competent. And that's when everything changes.

Chapter Ten

FROM THEORY TO ACTION

Meet Your VEM Toolkit

J ason sat in my chair looking absolutely defeated.

"I've been staring at a blank Word document for three days," he said. "I'm supposed to write a CV, but I don't have anything to put on it. I've never had a job. I don't have experience. I don't even know where to start."

I've heard this story a hundred times. Bright kid, capable, willing to work, but completely paralyzed by the blank page.

"What if I told you," I said, "that you could have a professional CV done in fifteen minutes?"

He looked at me like I'd just told him the earth was flat.

"There's no way," he said. "My careers advisor said it takes weeks to get it right."

"That's the old way," I told him. "Let me show you the new way."

I pulled out my phone and opened JumpstartCareers.co.uk. "This is what I've been building for the last few years. It's everything we've talked about, the Volume Experience Method, the P.O.P Algorithm, the power of 'yet', but turned into a system that actually works in the real world."

Jason looked skeptical, but he leaned in.

"Here's how it works," I said. "You answer some questions about yourself, school projects, volunteering, part-time work, even hobbies. The AI takes what you tell it and translates it into professional language. No blank page. No staring at the screen wondering what to write. Just answer the questions, and it builds your CV for you."

"That sounds too easy," he said.

"It is easy," I said. "That's the point. We've been making this harder than it needs to be."

Jason signed up right there in the chair. Fifteen minutes later, he had a CV. A real, professional CV that highlighted his volunteer work at a youth club, his role organizing a school fundraiser, and his part-time babysitting experience, all translated into skills employers actually care about: communication, organization, reliability, problem-solving.

He stared at his phone. "I can't believe I've been putting this off for three days. This took fifteen minutes."

"Exactly," I said. "And now you can start applying. Because that's where the real work begins."

Two months later, Jason came back with a job offer. But more than that, he came back with confidence. He'd sent over sixty applications, had twelve interviews, and learned exactly what he wanted. He didn't just get *a* job, he got the *right* job.

That's what the platform does. It removes the barriers that keep young people stuck, and it gives them the tools to implement VEM in the real world.

Let me show you how.

The Five Pillars of VEM Toolkit - Your complete career development system

The Five Pillars: Your VEM Toolkit

When I built JumpstartCareers.co.uk, I had one goal: **Turn VEM theory into practical action.**

Because theory is useless if you can't apply it. And most young people don't need more advice,they need a system that actually works.

So I built five pillars. Five tools that work together to take you from "I don't know where to start" to "I've got multiple offers and I'm choosing the best one."

Here's how it works.

Pillar 1: The AI-Powered CV Builder — The 15-Minute Revolution

The biggest barrier to job searching isn't lack of ability. It's a blank page.

You sit down to write a CV, and you freeze. What should I write? How do I say it? What if it's not good enough?

So you spend days,sometimes weeks,agonizing over every word. And in the meantime, you're not applying. You're stuck.

The AI-Powered CV Builder solves that.

Here's how it works: You log in, and the platform asks you a series of simple questions.

- *What school projects have you worked on?*

- *Have you done any volunteering?*

- *Do you have any part-time work experience?*

- *What hobbies or interests do you have?*

- *What skills have you learned in school or outside of it?*

You answer in plain English. No fancy language. No professional jargon. Just honest answers.

Then the AI takes what you've written and translates it into professional CV language. For example:

You write: "I helped organize a bake sale at school to raise money for charity. We made £300."

The AI translates: "Coordinated fundraising event, managing logistics, volunteer scheduling, and financial tracking, resulting in £300 raised for charitable causes. Demonstrated organizational skills, teamwork, and initiative."

See the difference? You're not lying. You're not exaggerating. You're just presenting your experience in the language employers understand.

And it takes fifteen minutes.

Jason wasn't unique. I've watched hundreds of young people go from "I have nothing to put on my CV" to "I've got a professional CV ready to send" in less time than it takes to watch an episode of their favorite show.

That's the 15-minute revolution. And it changes everything.

Because once you've got a CV, you can start applying. And once you start applying, you're in the game.

Pillar 2: The Volume Application System – Swipe Right on Your Future

Alright, you've got a CV. Now what?

Most job boards are overwhelming. Thousands of listings. Complicated filters. You spend an hour searching and end up more confused than when you started.

The Volume Application System is different.

It's designed like a dating app,because that's what works for this generation. You see a job. You swipe right if you're interested. You swipe left if you're not.

But here's the key: **The platform tracks your volume.**

Remember, the VEM philosophy is ten applications per week. That's the baseline. That's what creates options.

So the platform shows you exactly how many applications you've sent this week. It gamifies the process. You get a progress bar. You get notifications. You get a little dopamine hit every time you hit your target.

And here's the best part: **The platform auto-fills your application.**

You've already entered your information once,your CV, your contact details, your availability. So when you apply for a job, the platform fills in the forms for you. One click, and you're done.

No more copying and pasting the same information into twenty different application forms. No more spending an hour per application.

You can genuinely send ten applications in thirty minutes.

That's how you create volume without burning out.

Pillar 3: The Mock Interview AI – Practice Without the Pressure

Here's the thing about interviews: Most people are terrible at them the first time. And the second time. And the third time.

Not because they're not capable, but because they haven't practiced.

You wouldn't expect someone to play a piano recital without practicing. You wouldn't expect someone to run a marathon without training. But we expect young people to walk into interviews,high-pressure, high-stakes situations,with zero practice.

That's insane.

The Mock Interview AI solves that.

Here's how it works: You select a job you're applying for. The AI generates realistic interview questions based on that specific role and company. You record your answers on your phone or computer. The AI analyzes your response and gives you instant feedback.

- *Did you answer the question directly?*

- *Did you give specific examples?*

- *Did you speak clearly and confidently?*

- *Did you use filler words like "um" or "like" too much?*

You get a score. You get suggestions for improvement. And then you try again.

You can do this as many times as you want. No judgment. No pressure. Just practice.

And here's the bonus: **The platform researches the company for you.**

It pulls information from the company's website, reviews, and social media. It tells you what the company values, what their culture is like, what questions they're likely to ask.

So when you walk into the real interview, you're not guessing. You're prepared.

I've watched kids go from stumbling over their words in the first mock interview to delivering confident, polished answers by the tenth. And that confidence shows up in the real interviews.

Pillar 4: The Online Presence Builder – Your 24/7 Job Interview

Here's something most young people don't realize: **Employers Google you.**

Before they invite you for an interview, they're looking you up online. They're checking your social media. They're seeing what comes up when they search your name.

And if what they find is a bunch of dodgy photos from a party two years ago, or a Twitter account full of complaints, or nothing at all,that's a problem.

Your online presence is your 24/7 job interview. And most young people have no idea how to manage it.

The Online Presence Builder walks you through it step by step.

- *How to set up a professional LinkedIn profile, even if you have no experience.*

- *How to clean up your social media so it works for you, not against you.*

- *How to create a simple personal website or portfolio if you want to go the extra mile.*

- *How to make sure the first thing employers see when they Google you is something impressive.*

It's not about being fake or pretending to be someone you're not. It's about presenting your authentic self in a professional way.

And it works. I've seen kids get interview requests just because their LinkedIn profile showed up in a recruiter's search.

Pillar 5: The Progress Dashboard – Gamify Your Growth

Here's the problem with traditional job searching: It's demotivating.

You send applications and hear nothing. You go to interviews and get rejected. You feel like you're working hard, but you've got nothing to show for it.

The Progress Dashboard changes that.

It tracks everything:

- *How many applications you've sent this week.*

- *How many responses you've received.*

- *How many interviews you've completed.*

- *How many offers you've got.*

- *What your "hit rate" is, the percentage of applications that lead to interviews.*

But here's the key: **It celebrates effort, not just outcomes.**

You get points for sending applications. You get badges for hitting your weekly target. You get progress bars that fill up as you move through the process.

Because here's the truth: You can't control whether an employer says yes. But you can control how many applications you send. You can control how much you practice. You can control your effort.

And when you see that effort visualized, when you see the numbers going up, the progress bars filling, the badges unlocking, it keeps you motivated.

It reminds you that you're not stuck. You're moving forward.

How It All Works Together

Alright, let me show you what this looks like in practice.

You sign up for JumpstartCareers.co.uk. You spend fifteen minutes building your CV using the AI tool. You've got a professional CV ready to go.

You open the Volume Application System. You swipe through jobs. You find ten that look interesting. You apply to all ten in thirty minutes because the platform auto-fills your information.

You get three interview requests. You use the Mock Interview AI to practice. You do five mock interviews for each company. By the time the real interview comes, you're calm and confident.

You check the company research the platform provides. You know what they value. You know what questions they're likely to ask. You walk in prepared.

You nail the interview. You get an offer.

You repeat the process. You get more offers. Now you've got options.

You use the VEM Options Matrix to evaluate them. You choose the one that fits your priorities.

You've gone from "I don't know where to start" to "I'm choosing between multiple offers" in six to eight weeks.

That's the power of the platform. It doesn't replace the human element, it amplifies your authentic self.

What This Means for You

For teens:

Stop overthinking. Stop waiting for the perfect moment. Just sign up, build your CV, and start applying. The platform will guide you through every step.

Use the tools. Do the mock interviews. Track your progress. Celebrate the small wins. You're building skills that'll serve you for life.

For parents:

The platform gives you visibility without takeover. You can see your teen's progress,how many applications they've sent, how many interviews they've done,without micromanaging. You can support without controlling.

Encourage them to use the tools. Celebrate their effort. And trust the process.

For educators:

The platform is designed to integrate with your careers program. You can track your students' progress. You can see who's applying, who's stuck, who needs extra support.

It gives you data. It gives you outcomes. It proves your career program works.

Technology doesn't replace the human element. It amplifies your authentic self.

And when you combine VEM theory with the right tools, you don't just get a job.

You get options. You get confidence. You get control over your future.

Let me show you how.

Your Next Steps: How to Get Started Today

Alright, we've covered a lot. Theory, stories, data, tools. But none of it matters if you don't take action.

So here's what you do next.

For Teens:

Go to jumpstartcareers.co.uk and sign up. It's free to start.

Build your CV using the AI-Powered CV Builder. 15 minutes. Do it today.

Set your weekly target: 10 applications per week. Put it in your calendar.

Do your first mock interview. Just one. See how it feels.

Send your first application. Don't overthink it. Just send it.

That's it. Five steps. You can do all of them today.

And once you've done them, keep going. Ten applications per week. Track your progress. Practice your interviews. Learn from your rejections.

Within 6-8 weeks, you'll have options. And options change everything.

For Parents:

Talk to your teen about VEM. Share this book with them.

Encourage them to sign up for the platform. Offer to help if they want it, but don't take over.

Shift your focus from outcomes to effort. Ask, "How many applications did you send this week?" not "Have you heard back yet?"

Celebrate the reps. Every application, every mock interview, every rejection bounced back from,those are wins.

Trust the process. Volume works. Practice works. They'll get there.

For Educators:

Explore jumpstartcareers.co.uk for schools. We offer free trials and training.

Integrate VEM into your careers program. Set class targets. Track progress. Celebrate effort.

Normalize rejection. Teach students that "no" is data, not defeat.

Measure outcomes. Show your leadership that your careers program actually works.

Join the VEM community. Connect with other schools using the method. Share what works.

The Final Word: Every "No" Is Training for Your Eventual "Yes"

I've been cutting hair for 34 years. I've had thousands of conversations with young people who felt stuck, defeated, and hopeless.

And I've watched hundreds of them transform,not because they suddenly became more talented or more confident, but because they learned a simple truth:

You don't need to be perfect. You just need to start.

Send the applications. Do the practice interviews. Track your progress. Learn from your rejections. Create options. Make decisions. Own your future.

That's VEM. That's the method. That's the path.

And it works.

Not because I'm some genius who figured out a secret. But because I listened. I watched. I learned from the young people who came through my door. I saw what worked and what didn't. And I built a system around it.

Now it's your turn.

Stop waiting. Stop perfecting. Stop hoping for the right opportunity to appear.

Start applying. Start practicing. Start building.

Because every "no" is training for your eventual "yes."

And the future belongs to those who learn to turn "no" into "not yet" into "yes."

So go. Sign up. Build your CV. Send your first application.

Your future is waiting.

And it starts today.

THE END

ABOUT THE AUTHOR

A BOUT THE AUTHOR

Errol Lloyd Jones is a 34-year veteran barber and the founder of the Volume Experience Method (VEM), a revolutionary approach to youth career development. Through thousands of conversations in his barber shop, Errol discovered that traditional career advice was failing young people,and he set out to create a better way.

Combining real-world experience with psychological research from Albert Bandura and Carol Dweck, Errol developed VEM: a system that teaches young people to create options through volume, build confidence through practice, and make strategic decisions based on their priorities.

His digital platform, jumpstartcareers.co.uk, has helped thousands of young people across the UK secure employment, build confidence, and take control of their futures. Errol's work has been adopted by schools, praised by parents, and celebrated by the young people whose lives have been transformed by his method.

This is his first book.

RESOURCES

Jumpstartcareers.co.uk – The VEM digital platform with AI-powered CV builder, volume application system, mock interview AI, online presence builder, and progress dashboard.

Free Resources:

VEM Options Matrix template

Weekly application tracker

Interview question bank

LinkedIn profile checklist

For Schools:

Teacher training programs

Student implementation guides

Outcome tracking tools

VEM curriculum integration resources

Join the VEM Community:

Connect with other young people using VEM

Share success stories and lessons learned

Get support from peers and mentors

Access exclusive tips and updates

Visit jumpstartcareers.co.uk to get started today.

Printed in Dunstable, United Kingdom

72310501R00048